Contents

Family Lives

Website: www.familylives.org.uk

Helpline: 0808 800 2222

Contact a Family

Helpline: 0808 808 3555

cafamily.org.uk

YoungMinds

Helpline: 0808 802 5544

youngminds.org.uk

Kids Behaviour

kidsbehaviour.co.uk

Respect

Helpline: 0808 802 4040

What is conduct disorder?

Conduct disorder is a mental disorder diagnosed in childhood or adolescence. The most potent characteristic of conduct disorder is a consistent routine of behaviour by a child or teenager in which the simple rights of individuals are denied and rules or social norms are broken.

These behaviours are commonly referred to as "antisocial behaviours." These behaviours fall into four main categories:

- Aggressive conduct
- Non-aggressive action
- Deceitfulness or theft
- Breaking of norms repeatedly.

Symptoms of conduct disorder

Aggression towards people and animals - Destruction of Property

- Physically cruel to animals
- Physically cruel to people
- Raped somebody
- Robbed somebody
- Used a dangerous item that can cause injury
- Usually sparks physical outbursts
- Often annoys, threatens or scares others

Deceitfulness or Theft

- Has gone into someone else's house, building or car without permission
- Has taken objects of high value without asking the owner
- Usually lies to avoid obligations or to get things

Serious Violations of Rules

- Usually stays out at night despite parental rules, starting before thirteen years old
- Has ran away from home overnight at least twice while living with parents / carer or once without returning for a long period of time
- Often skipping school, beginning before thirteen years old

Conduct disorder poem

Yes, I pushed my dog down the stairs.

Yes, I pulled out my sister's hair.

Yes, I kicked my grandmother's chair, just as she was about to sit there.

I don't feel guilty, I don't care.

I would do it again.

The 2 sub-sections of conduct disorder

Childhood-Onset Type:

This sub-group is defined by the onset of at least one factor of conduct disorder prior to the age ten. People with childhood-onset type are normally male and they usually have interrupted peer relationships, show physical aggression towards other people and may have had Oppositional Defiant Disorder during early childhood. People with this type usually have symptoms that meet full criteria for conduct disorder before they start puberty. These individuals are more likely to have constant conduct disorder that grows into adult Antisocial Personality Disorder than are those with Adolescent-Onset Type.

Adolescent-Onset Type:

This sub-group is defined by the lack of any criteria factor of conduct disorder before the age of ten years. In comparison to those with the childhood-onset type, these people are not as likely to show aggressive behaviours and tend to have more normal peer relationships. The ratio of males to females with conduct disorder is narrower for the adolescent-onset type than for the childhood-onset type. These individuals are less fitted to have consistent conduct disorder or grow into adult Antisocial Personality Disorder.

Other problems

Oppositional defiant disorder and ADHD often occur within individuals with conduct disorder. Some other disorders that may occur with conduct disorder include:

- Anxiety disorders
- Bipolar disorders
- Depressive
- Specific learning disorder
- Substance use disorders

How conduct disorder is diagnosed

Conduct disorder is diagnosed by a persistent routine of behaviour in which the simple rights of individuals, regulations or other age-suitable societal norms are broken, shown with the presence of three or more of the below listed events in the past year, with at least one event occurring within the past six months:

- Physically cruel to animals
- Physically cruel to people
- Committed rape
- Committed robbery

- Used a dangerous item that can cause injury
- Usually sparks physical outbursts
- Often annoys, threatens, or scares others
- Has gone into someone else's house, building, or car without permission
- Has taken objects of large value without asking the owner
- Usually does not tell the truth to avoid obligations or to get things
- Usually stays out at night despite parental rules, starting before thirteen years old
- Has ran away from home overnight at least twice while living with parents / carer or once without returning for a long period of time
- Often skipping school, beginning before thirteen years old

Accessing help

Listed below are some ways to access treatment:

- **See your GP**
- **Free NHS therapy services**. If you live in the United Kingdom
- **Specialist organisations**
- **Private psychotherapy**

A professional will talk with parents, teachers and other adults involved in the individual's life to rule out other possible causes.

Ned's story

From being a baby Ned seemed to be a little angrier than his older brother Simon was at that age. He didn't sleep as well as Simon did at his age and this was the conclusion his parents came to for him being more demanding.

At the age of two years old when Ned started to socialise more with other children his age, it became apparent that something was different.

He would constantly push the other children over, destroy every other child's toys and if ever he was confronted about his actions he would throw hour's long tantrums.

It seemed like Ned would throw multiple tantrums a day filled with violence towards anyone around him.

His parents started to get increasingly worried when Ned's violence became out of hand and uncontrollable. He started to punch, kick, bite and push his older brother Simon and the family dog Dino for no apparent reason or because of a slight inconvenience.

His outbursts became extremely worrying for his parents as they weren't sure if he felt any remorse at all for his actions.

Everyone walked on eggshells around Ned; they didn't want to trigger another episode.

When Ned was 8 years old he got kicked out of school due to his behaviour. Ned would tell you he didn't like school anyways.

He was violent towards the staff and pupils and would destroy anything he could see. His teacher had previously talked to his parents stating that this wasn't normal behaviour and that maybe they should seek help.

Ned's parents wanted to get help for him but were too scared, ashamed and embarrassed to ask for any.

His behaviour increasingly made the atmosphere of the family home more hostile.

He would often run away from home for hours or even overnight in one case with no trace causing mass panic for his family.

Ned's parents would try to punish him by confiscating his toys but he would always find a way to steal them back.

Three months later and Ned's parents were mortified when they found that he had killed their neighbour's cat. "Why are you doing these things?" Ned's mother asked with a tear in her eye. Ned began on a violence filled episode punching and kicking his parents and smashing any objects that were in his surroundings, threatening their lives. Ned didn't seem to be remorseful of his actions at all.

September 25th 2014. This is when Ned's parents decided it was time to reach out for help. His mother had already done a thorough research for psychotherapists and boot camps for Ned in the past.

Ned's parents eventually came to the conclusion that it was best to take him to a psychotherapist.

Whilst at the psychotherapist's office, Ned's parents had to fill out a form. This form asked questions about Ned's behaviour and his day to day life.

After talking with Ned's parents and a few visits home to see Ned and view his behaviour, the doctor diagnosed him with conduct disorder (CD) and prescribed him with some medication.

Ned was enrolled into a school for individuals with developmental and behavioural problems. A school with trained staff for children with similar issues, and a smaller pupil to teacher ratio.

Ned attended this school for 4 years and the school was doing wonders for him but unfortunately as he got older and stronger he became harder to control.

His strength was increasing with his age and in turn made him almost impossible to control and once again Ned was kicked out of school.

His parents once again reached out for advice, they were informed that even with therapy there is a high chance that Ned will live a life institutionalised.

They proceeded with the intense therapy; it had come out in a therapy session that Ned had killed more than just the neighbour's cat in his life. He had killed rabbits and he had even killed a stray dog. Ned had disclosed that he could just kill his family if they annoy him.

July 5th 2019 Ned was caught raping a neighbour's child, after he was beaten almost to death by the father of the child he was sent to a youth detention centre. This is where he spent the rest of his childhood.

Ned's parents cut ties with him after this horrific incident.

Whilst in the youth detention centre Ned displayed acts of severe violence almost killing many others around him. He was transferred to prison after his 18th birthday.

Ned is still incarcerated to this day and frequently in isolation for his behaviour.

Conduct disorder poem

Punch, punch, punch

Bite, bite, bite

I'll go where I want all day all night.

Don't tell me what to do and don't make me do something I don't like. I'll teach you not to do that alright.

References

- Nip in the Bud. (n.d.). *Where to go for help*. [online] Available at: https://nipinthebud.org/where-to-go-for-help/#conduct [Accessed 13 Apr. 2021].
- Pietro, S. (2016). *Conduct Disorder Basics*. [online] Child Mind Institute. Available at: https://childmind.org/guide/guide-to-conduct-disorder/.
- Harvard Health Publishing (2011). *Options for managing conduct disorder - Harvard Health*. [online] Harvard Health. Available at: https://www.health.harvard.edu/newsletter_article/options-for-managing-conduct-disorder.

Personal notes: